T0134799

Africa for Kids

Pene and John Cleaves

Hi,

This is a picture of us, Pene and John, we love this beautiful country, South Africa, and the wonderful wildlife.

We always have a fantastic time, going on safaris to see the animals, or visiting the school and helping to provide equipment and support to them. One of our most amazing days this time was a brilliant day when we went canoeing, the hippos and crocodiles were all around us. Further on near the river entrance we found a family of elephants on the edge of the lake, they had lots of little elephants but especially exciting was seeing the twin elephant babies who were only 6months old.

We are happy just looking around either from the safari vehicle, walking or canoeing with our guides.

We have made some very good friends over here and everyone makes us feel very welcome and we feel it is our home from home. We would like to share our story with you, we hope you enjoy it.

Xxxooo

"It would be really nice to go and see all our friends in Africa again." said John "That's a great idea," said Pene "let's go soon."

The days past by quicker and quicker and then at last the big day arrived.

"Are we all packed John? the taxi will be here soon" asked Pene "I am getting excited". "Yes, all done, have you got the passports and tickets?" John replied.

"I have got all that in my bag don't worry, there is the taxi now" said Pene.

After a long flight across Australia and then the Indian Ocean we arrived in Durban, picked up the car and headed off. We whizzed along the road, eager to see all our friends again. "Oh no! look at all the goats and chickens on the road hope they move quickly so we can keep going" said Pene.

"Look that is the school, we must be nearly at the lodge" said John "and there's the gate". We drove down the rough road to the entrance and our friends Adriaan, Heike, Erica, Brett, Ruan, Mitch, George and the lovely girls who look after us were there to greet us. "It feels like coming home" Pene laughed.

We hurriedly unpacked and had a lovely tea and then jumped in the jeep for a quick ride to see if any black rhino were around. We found a female and her calf on the hill, and then we started back as it was getting dark - we heard a rustle in the bushes, and in the jeep's, light saw a big male watching us. After we got home, we were very tired from our busy day, so we went to bed; as we wanted to be up early to go and visit the children at the school.

On our way to the school we saw some female white rhinos and their babies on the side of the road. "Did you know the main difference between black and white rhino is their mouth?" asked John. "I think I read somewhere that the name for the white rhino originally meant wide mouth, so I think they have the wider mouth, is that right?" asked Pene, "and they are slightly bigger than the black rhino".

"Yes, and the white rhino grazes on the grass and the black rhino plucks the berries and leaves off the bushes with their lips" replied John, "Also the black rhino babies follow their mums and the white rhino baby runs ahead".

White Rhinoceros - wide mouth - walk with their head down

Black Rhinoceros - smaller with hooked top lip walk with their head up

We visited the school and took the children some books to read, they were fascinated with the different animals in the books and we had great fun showing them which were Australian, and which were African animals. The children thought a picture of Pene with a snake was a bit scary, but it was only a carpet python and quite harmless.

On the second day the children sang for us, we did not understand the words, but it was beautiful, the children had lovely voices and sang in harmony together.

"I had tears in my eyes it was so lovely" said Pene.

"I wonder who is having the best breakfast, the little humming bird with his nectar, or the dark-capped bulbul on our breakfast table? Oh, now the bulbul is having a shower under the hose" said John. "We had so much fun at the school yesterday, what shall we do today?" asked Pene

"I know," said John "why don't we get a picnic and go to the waterhole, maybe the birds will be out playing in the water, they are so pretty and fun to watch?".

We packed a picnic and off we went. We were sitting quietly at the waterhole, and very soon a little brown hooded kingfisher came out of a hole in the bank and flew to a branch in the middle of the water.

"One kingfisher looks like he is saying to the other 'Come on you can do it, there you go, told you so', to encourage the other to fly from the nest in the mud bank to the twig in the-waterhole" said John.

It was such a lovely day Brett suggested we go out on the boat onto the lake. "That is a brilliant idea" said John. We all climbed into the jeep and off we went. The jeep rattled and banged, jumped and bumped along the rough road, we had to hang on with all our might, but the seats were very slippery and as we slid along all our gear fell on the floor in a big heap. John nearly had to stand on his head to pick it all up!

At last we reached the lake and got on the boat. "Look at all the birds standing on that sandbank oh dear, we must have scared them, now there is only one left" said Pene. "He looks like he is walking on the water."

"The hornbill is looking for bugs, and a pretty green dove is watching it, maybe hoping he will drop a titbit for him, and look at the enormous wings on that fish eagle" exclaimed John "I wonder if he caught a fish?". "That makes me think of dinner" laughed Pene "time to go home".

Another lovely day and off in the jeep with Heike we go, along another bumpy road down near the lake. "Look there are lots of elephants coming out of the trees, I hope they come this way," said Pene "let's stay and watch while they play and cool off in the water". "I think the babies are watching and trying to copy the big boys play fight" laughed John.

"These elephants are at the drinking hole made especially for them, so they don't always have to go down to the lake to have a drink and cool down" said John.

"There are three different sized elephants all drinking together, you can see how tiny they are when they are babies and how big they grow, and this is not even a fully grown male here" said Pene.

"Look, all around on the ground there are dung beetles, which are not just black but a variety of bright colours, all being very busy," said John "They are very important for the animals as they break down the dung and use the nutrients to help more plants to grow so the animals have enough to eat" explained John.

"What are those strange plants there?" asked Pene. "They are fungi growing out of the dung that the beetles have left behind, it also helps break down the dung" replied John.

This baby seems to be having a wonderful time rolling the mud!

On the way back home, we saw another herd of elephants at the lake edge all getting a last-minute drink before heading back into the trees for the evening. "What a lovely sunset, a brilliant end to the day" said John. The baby at the front was a new calf we found and were privileged to name him "Virgo".

Can you see the twin babies having a drink they are so cute!! This water hole helps the babies get a drink while they learn to control their trunks!

Amazing sunset over the Jozini Dam

The next day we decided to go on the lake instead of watching from the shore and the boat. So, we went canoeing on the lake with Mitch and saw the hippopotamus and crocodiles - they were very close. "I think you better paddle John, I seem to be getting us stuck on the sandbank and we don't want to upset them, they are bigger than us!" said Pene.

There were lots of birds along the shore, egrets, cormorants and fish eagles; there we also lots of waterbuck and reedbuck in the reeds at the water edge, and the rhinos were out with their babies enjoying the sunshine.

"See the big hippo on the water edge he is very pink he looks like he is sunburnt on his face, and that little one thinks the boat float is a teething ring, I hope he does not swallow it" said Pene.

We went out for a ride in the jeep, as we drove around a bend in the road there was a troop of vervet monkeys scampering around and running in and out of the bushes. "Look at the monkeys high in the trees, why aren't they joining in with the others, playing on the road?" asked Pene. "They are the lookout, they will chatter if a leopard or an eagle is around so the monkeys and other animals can hide and not end up being dinner" replied John. "Look at the big monkey encouraging the little one to climb the tree, oh, look he is up swinging around by himself now. The baby just fell off his mum's back, hope she stops to pick him up," said Pene "that's good she has him now".

"Spy Cam is a very clever way to see the nocturnal animals that we would not normally catch sight of," said John "like the honey badger, aardvark, serval, leopard and a porcupine with her baby". "What is nocturnal?" asked Pene. "It means animals that prefer to come out at night for various reasons, like avoiding predators, or their eyes don't see very well during the day" replied John.

"The hyenas are having a great time in the water trough, and that bird looks like he is yelling at the warthog" laughed Pene. " I am glad I don't have to use the water for a bath or to drink after that crowd have been in there" said John

"Let's leave the monkeys to play, what is that in the bushes over there?" asked John. "It's lots of different antelopes and gazelles" replied Pene. We saw at least six different ones can you name the ones in the pictures, waterbuck, common eland, Thompson's gazelle, impala, kudu and grant's gazelle, and the little red and grey duikers, they are very shy, and we only saw one of each of those. "Did you notice some of the females have horns, but they are smaller than the males" said Pene "and others don't have any horns at all".

We went for a drive with Ruan and far away in the distance, we saw some heads moving above the prickly thorn trees. Then we saw they had very long legs, and very long necks, can you guess what they were? That's right giraffes. They are very graceful, have pretty faces and long blue tongues.

"How many can you see John?" asked Pene. "One, two, three and four giraffes - they are very inquisitive and will probably watch us for a while over the trees before coming in closer for a better look" replied John. "They are slowly coming over here now, there is one having a drink, he has a long way to get into the water, he must have good knees!" laughed Pene.

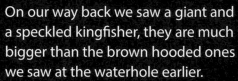

On our way back we saw a giant and a speckled kingfisher, they are much bigger than the brown hooded ones we saw at the waterhole earlier.

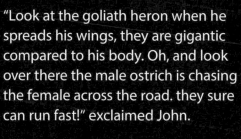

"Look at the goliath heron when he spreads his wings, they are gigantic compared to his body. Oh, and look over there the male ostrich is chasing the female across the road. they sure can run fast!" exclaimed John.

Back at the lodge we had afternoon tea in the garden. "John can you see that huge monitor lizard in the tree, he is hiding in the branches?" asked Pene "and the lilac roller on that old tree stump, they are really colourful aren't they".

"Yes, I see them " replied John "but I am watching the nyala in those bushes, he was watching me before coming over to drink from the bird bath, usually he drinks from the swimming pool! I think the females are enjoying the grass on the lawn outside our room" said John "while the warthogs are running around the grounds on the other side of the lodge".

It's very hot today I think the animals will be looking for somewhere cool to spend the day, it looks like that rhino has found a cool spot in the mud puddle, he doesn't look like he is planning on moving any time soon" said John.

"I think that elephant is trying to see what we are doing he is very close" said Pene "he does not seem bothered by us here in the vehicle".

"Can you see the lions over there on the rocks"? asked John. "Only just, with the binoculars, they are lying very still enjoying the sun on the rocks and probably the breeze off the water, I think" replied Pene.

Leopards are very hard to find as they are often in the trees, and if they drop their head or hide behind the branches, they are almost impossible to spot.

The Cheetah does not seem to mind us getting close we were very quiet, and he just lifted his head to look and went back to sleep! A cheetah has black markings on his face which help his eyes when he goes in for a kill as it absorbs the suns reflections on his face, and he can see better. Cheetahs kill during daylight and can run very fast for a short period and if he does not have time to recover and eat his kill, he may have to leave it, if other predators are around, as he expends all his energy in the run to catch his prey.

Lions are the laziest of the big cats and stay in a very small area, in a family group called a pride. The lioness' do most of the hunting but the male eats first!! They are very territorial and will chase off any other lions.

"The leopard tortoise seems to be playing hide and seek popping his head in and out - they have amazing patterns on their shells, which also can be "read" to see how old they are" said John.
"See the Samango monkey with her baby, there he goes running up the tree" said Pene. "I think mum is pretending to sleep, one minute her eyes are closed then she is looking at us again" laughed John "maybe she thinks we can't see her if her eyes are closed, like the kids when you play hide and seek".

"This zebra wants to get up close and personal, he is just about kissing the camera." laughed Pene "There is a very young baby he looks like a stuffed toy, so cute. The one in the road is just calmly watching us and in no hurry to let us drive on, if he doesn't move soon, we will miss our flight home and have to stay here!" said Pene.

"That's ok", laughed John "I'm sad we are leaving anyway". "Never mind, John I know we will be back again very soon" replied Pene.

On the way back to the airport, we climbed to the top of the hill to see this fabulous sunset over the mountains which was reflecting back onto the fig tree growing out of the rocks at the top of the look out. "It's beautiful, we must come back again soon, and keep our adventure going." said John

"I can't wait to come back and see all our friends, the animals, and the children, and to have more amazing adventures." said Pene.

Birds at sunset roosting in the tree for the night.

A Night Jar is very hard to get on camera as soon as they see lights they fly away!! They are nocturnal and eats bugs that fly at night.

Elephants still wander around at night they sleep for short periods often leaning against a tree or resting their trunk on the ground.

Balboa Press books may be ordered through booksellers or by contacting:

Balboa Press
A Division of Hay House
1663 Liberty Drive
Bloomington, IN 47403
www.balboapress.com.au
1 (877) 407-4847

ISBN: 978-1-5043-1751-1 (sc)
ISBN: 978-1-5043-1752-8 (e)

Print information available on the last page.

Balboa Press rev. date: 04/12/2019

BALBOA.
PRESS
A DIVISION OF HAY HOUSE

Printed in the United States
By Bookmasters